The Water Hole

For Bob

The Water Hole

Graeme Base

Down to the secret water hole the animals all come.
As seasons bring forth drought and flood, they gather there as one.
United in their common need, their numbers swell to ten—
But hidden deep among the trees lie ten times that again!

PUFFIN BOOKS

1

One Rhino

drinking at the water hole.

"Snort, splosh!"
(Mmm, delicious!)

2

Two Tigers
lapping at the water hole.

"Grrrrrr!"
(Goodness gracious, how very delectable!)

3

Three Toucans

squawking around the water hole.

"Ark, ark! Arrrk!"
(It's party time, fellas! Drink up!)

But something was happening . . .

Four Snow Leopards

gazing at the water hole.

"Prrrrrrr."

(Hmmm. We must be careful, brothers.)

The pool was getting smaller . . .

5

Five Moose

wallowing in the water hole.

"Moo, moo, moooooiii!"
(Hey, get your hoof out of my ear!)

. . . and smaller . . .

6

Six Catfish

floundering in the water hole.

"Blub, blub, blub!"
(Blub, blub, blub!)

. . . and smaller.

7

Seven Pandas

sipping at the water hole.

"Tsk, tsk, tsk."

(After you. No, no—I insist.)

Eight Ladybugs
meeting by the water hole.

"Bzui."

(So in conclusion, ladies and gentlebugs, I propose
we establish a sub-committee to report on the water level
crisis before the end of the fiscal year.
All in favor say bzui.)

Nine Tortoises

lumbering around the water hole.

"Scrmph, scrmph, scrmph."
(Okay, which of you wise guys hid all the water?)

10

Ten Kangaroos

looking at the water hole.

There was nothing to say.
The water was all gone.

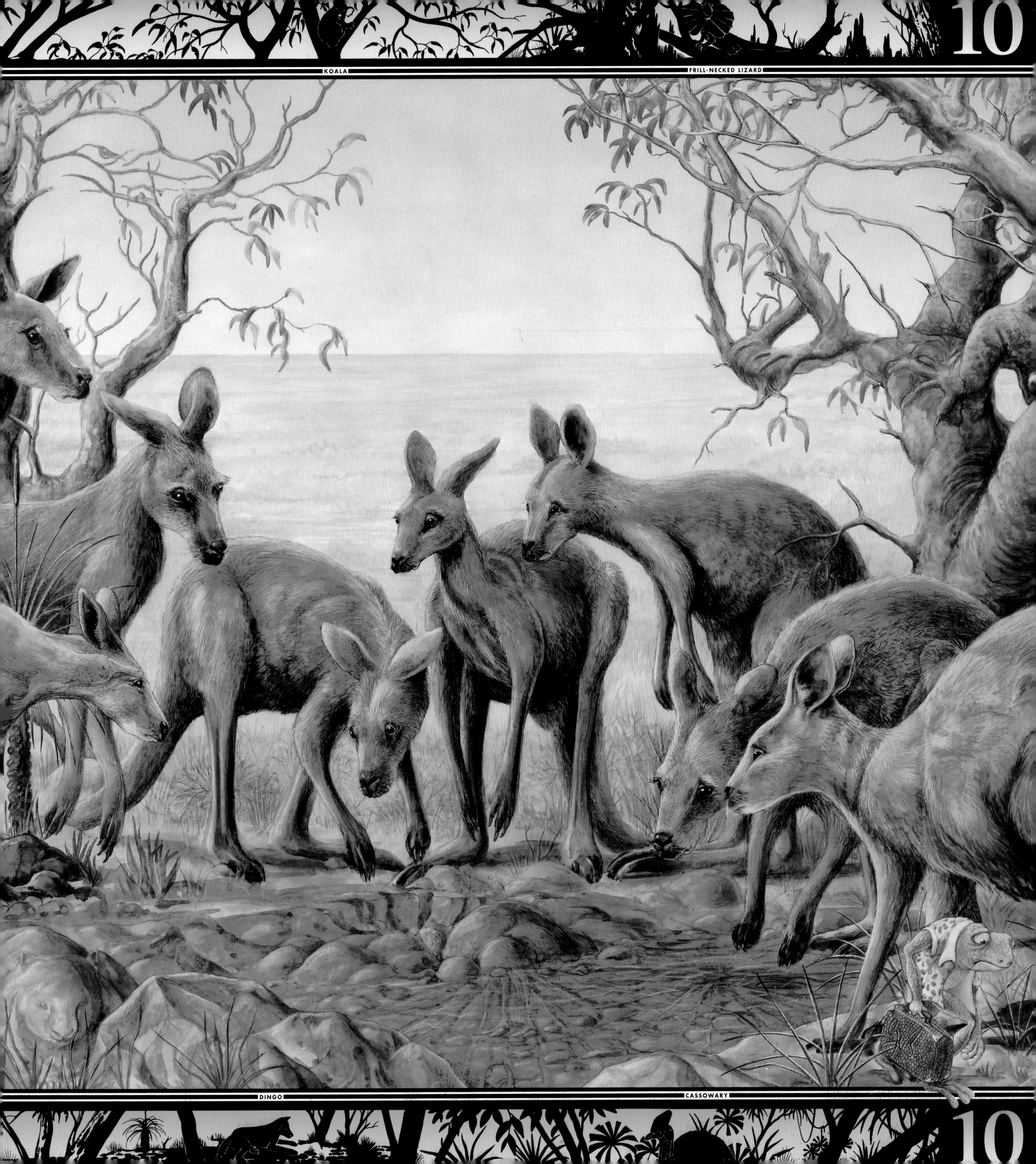
KOALA
FRILL-NECKED LIZARD
DINGO
CASSOWARY

And all the animals went away.

GREAT AUK
DODO
THYLACINE (TASMANIAN WOLF)

PASSENGER PIGEON
ROUND ISLAND BOA
DUSKY SPARROW

Then a shadow fell across the sun.

Clouds began to gather.

A single drop of rain fell.

It rained and rained and rained and rained . . .

And all the animals came back!

"Ooola! Oooya! Wahoooo!"
(Yippee!)